The Greek File

Images from a Mythic Land

William Abranowicz

Introduction by Edmund Keeley

RIZZOLI
NEW YORK

This book is dedicated to my mother, Margaret Meyer, who gave me life and held her family together so gallantly; to my wife, Andrea Raisfeld, who shared unequaled passion, knowledge, and love through this journey and gave life to our magnificent young Grecophiles, Zander, Simon, and Max Athena; and to my friend, Nadia Psychas, who quickly adopted me and made sure I kept coming back.

Introduction

Almost thirty years after his 1939 trip to Greece, Henry Miller offered a still valid generalization about encountering the country that is the subject of these brilliant photographs: "To know [Greece] thoroughly is impossible; to understand it requires genius; to fall in love with it is the easiest thing in the world. It is like falling in love with one's own divine image reflected in a thousand dazzling facets." As Miller himself exemplifies in his *The Colossus of Maroussi*, the secret for the artist, after having so easily fallen in love with the country, is to transform his divine self-image into a more universal representation that can touch others: both those who may know the artist's source and those ready to explore it. William Abranowicz succeeds in this transformation as Henry Miller did, but very much in his own mode. The personal understanding and love of which Miller speaks are clearly manifest in Abranowicz's image of the country in this collection, an image reflecting the many dazzling facets that he has discovered in the landscape, the seascape, the villages and the daily life of their inhabitants in contemporary Greece from 1988 to 1998. But his selection of things to illustrate what he has discovered and his creative use of the camera to bring these things to life in his own style have transformed the personal into the representative, and beyond that, into the kind of enduring statement that only the best art can provide.

Abranowicz's focus remains consistently on the islands of the Aegean, Santorini most of all, but also generously on Naxos, Patmos, Tinos, Sifnos, Aegina, and a fewer lesser known islands such as Karpathos, Thasos, Symi, and Halki. Yet what he offers us are rarely portraits of the islands as one would find them in a travel book; he avoids the tourist trail and follows the kind of path toward discovery that Lawrence Durrell pointed to when he first journeyed to Greece by sea from Italy: "You enter Greece as one might enter a dark crystal; the form of things becomes irregular, refracted." The refraction is apparent here in a number of startling instances, and rather than grand wide-angle representations of islands in the hot or dying sun, the emphasis is usually on the telling detail, the partial image, the encounter with new textures in a face or a fresco or a tapestry or what would be the simplest of objects were it not for the mystery that the camera discovers in each of them and reveals to us by isolating the objects in a particular way: a shirt or sweater, a rock cluster, a stone or metal staircase, glasses on a marble table, fish heads rising out of a basket of ice cubes, forks like flowers in a caddy, white sheets on a line billowing out against the dusk, votive offerings dangling over a saint's wounded features.

There is one photograph taken on the most popular of tourist islands, Mykonos, but not the Mykonos of windmills and white-washed churches seen from the cruise ship deck. What we find here is a still life of fruit and a carnation in a vase, framed by a swirling pattern of partially shuttered light. And when he takes us to what would seem to be his favorite island, Santorini, an example of what his camera selects is not the familiar picture of mules climbing the winding trail up the island's main cliff (a means of transport now challenged by a finicular) but a portrait of a single mule's white flank gently rippled like a segment of some quiet sea.

Another mode of imparting new and longer life to what could have been merely familiar arrives here in the cunning juxtaposition of images to highlight their hidden relationship. On facing pages we are given a candle-lit icon of an angelic figure from an Aegina shrine and a pendant bearing the Holy Virgin on the hirsute chest of a Patmos believer. In a four-part series, we encounter a fresco on Patmos that places a robed saint beside a bare-chested figure in a loin cloth presumably awaiting baptism, and this is followed in turn by two contemporary bathers entering the waters of Patmos to "baptize [themselves] anew in the raw," as Miller once put it. In another series, luscious grapes in baskets and on the vine are juxtaposed with a plate of grapes on a sun-dappled table. And when the world of ancient Greece makes a rare appearance in the form of a single austere column against the sky on the sacred island of Delos, it is preceded by a jetty of wooden slats against the sea on the sacred island of Patmos.

Like some of the more sensitive Hellenic and Philhellenic artists of our day, William Abranowicz is a student of the Greek light, that sometimes illusive yet pervasive attribute that perhaps defines the country's visual particularity. The Nobel laureate George Seferis sensed a process of humanization in the Greek light, yet his poetry speaks of that same light as both angelic and black. The English novelist John Fowles see this light as supremely beautiful but also hostile, engendering both passion and terror. And the painter Hadjikyriako-Ghika finds the light at the sun's meridian an unbearable brilliance, its reflection off sharp-edged stones, lanceolate leaves, and the acute angles of buildings an incandescent haze that makes the air seem to dance like a flame. One can discover any number of representations of this paradoxical intensity in this collection, especially effective in black and white prints. There are moments of off-white on off-white, of rooms where a slant of light appears to wash out the shadows around it, of light striking an unlit cigarette to create a shadow five times the cigarette's measure, of white villages floodlit by sunlight or halfway parted from their whiteness at the sun's discretion, and walls or stairways darkly decorated by the sun's handiwork through lattices or unseen passages. Among the more startling moments are those when the sun has turned its darker side to the earth and the moon is allowed to exercise its creative force. As though akin to the puppet master of the shadow theater shown here manipulating a Karaghiozi figure behind his brilliant screen, the moon appears in several of these photographs to create an image of a dark figure or cloud group or land mass set within or against its theatrical spread of light.

Lawrence Durrell, in tune with his friend Henry Miller, tells us that the Greek journey is first of all one that offers you the possibility of discovering yourself. If that is so—and I am one who thinks it is—these photographs provide ample ground for the reader to begin that journey in a most illuminating if vicarious way, or in the case of the lucky ones who have experienced that discovery, to arouse their nostalgia for the journey already made. In either case, the gift of this collection should be gratefully acknowledged.

—Edmund Keeley

I choose this image at random but how appropriate and accurate it is! When I think of Katsimbalis bending over to pick a flower from the bare soil of Attica the whole Greek world, past, present and future, rises before me. I see again the soft, low mounds in which the illustrious dead were hidden away; I see the violent light in which the stiff scrub, the worn rocks, the huge boulders of the dry river beds gleam like mica; I see the miniature islands floating above the surface of the sea, ringed with dazzling white bands; I see the eagles swooping out from the dizzy crags of inaccessible mountain tops, their sombre shadows slowly staining the bright carpet of earth below; I see the figures of solitary men trailing their flocks over the naked spine of the hills and the fleece of their beasts all golden fuzz as in the days of legend; I see the women gathered at the wells amidst the olive groves, their dress, their manners, their talk no different now than in Biblical times; I see the grand patriarchal figure of the priest, the perfect blend of male and female, his countenance serene, frank, full of peace and dignity;

I see the geometrical pattern of nature expounded by the earth itself in silence which is deafening. The Greek earth opens before me like the Book of Revelation. I never knew that the earth contains so much; I had walked blindfolded, with faltering, hesitant steps; I was proud and arrogant, content to live the false, restricted life of the city man. The light of Greece opened my eyes, penetrated my pores, expanded my whole being. I came home to the world, having found the true center and the real meaning of revolution. No warring conflicts between the nations of the earth can disturb this equilibrium. Greece herself may become embroiled, as we ourselves are now becoming embroiled, but I refuse categorically to become anything less than the citizen of the world which I silently declared myself to be when I stood in Agamemnon's tomb. From that day forth my life was dedicated to the recovery of the divinity of man. Peace to all men, I say, and life more abundant!

—Henry Miller
  From *The Colossus of Maroussi*

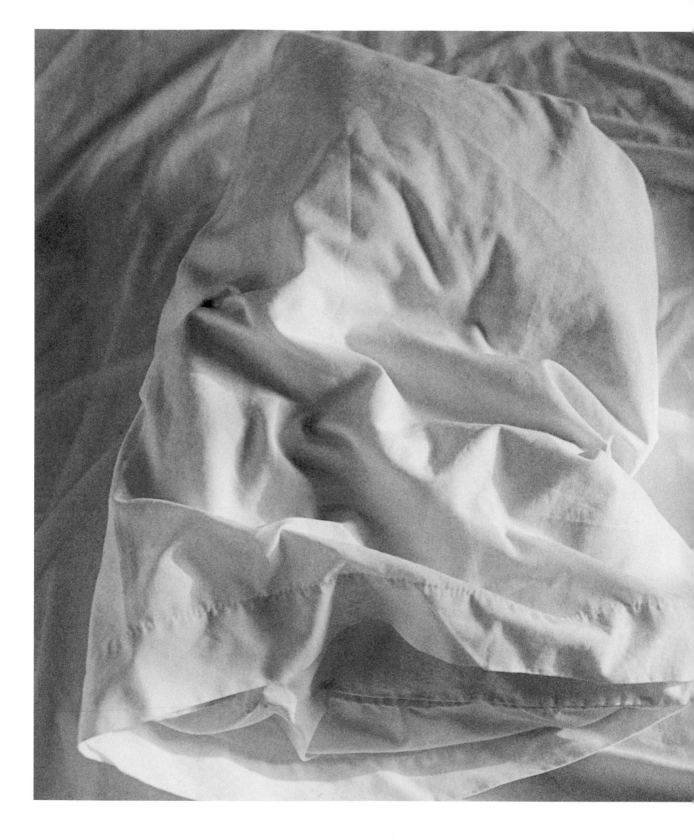

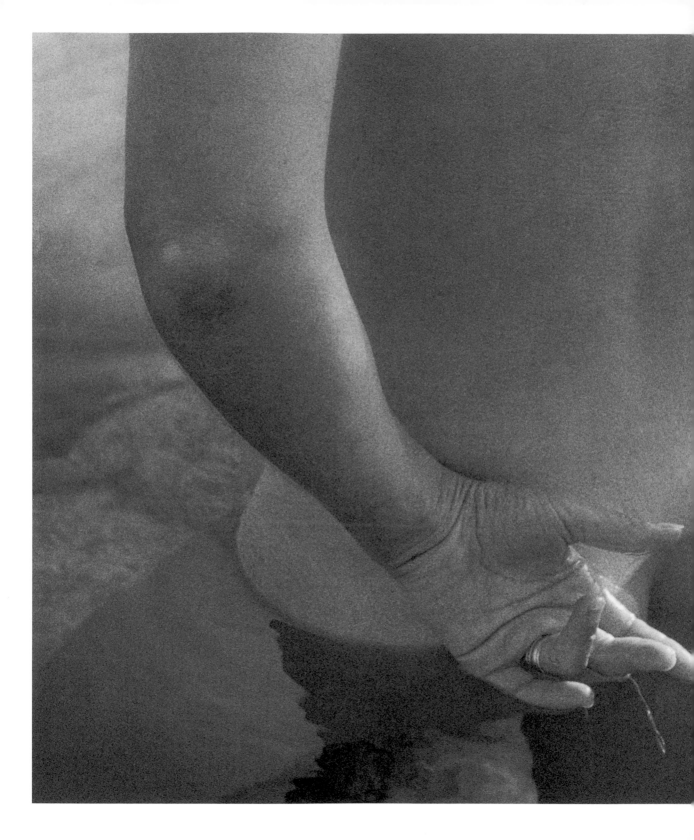

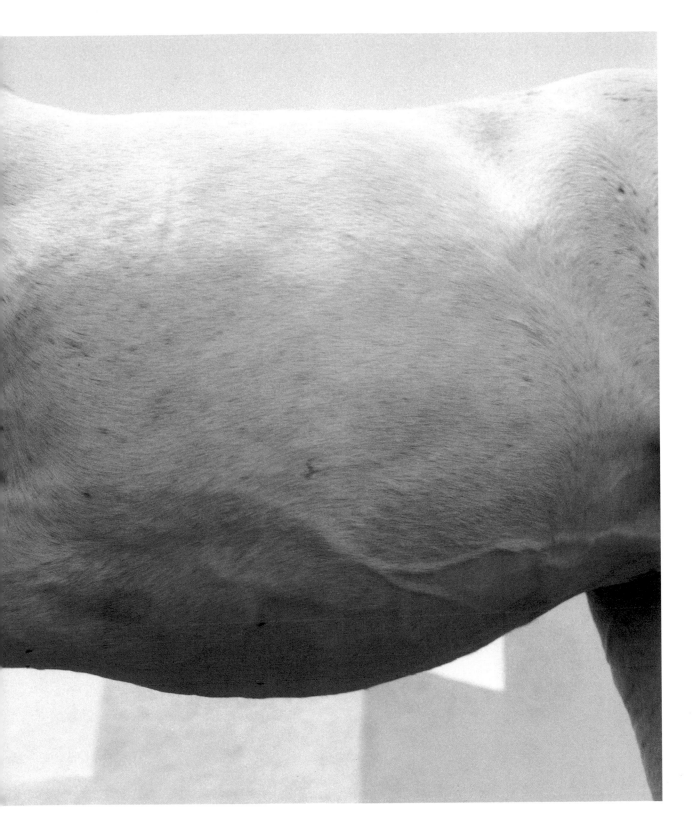

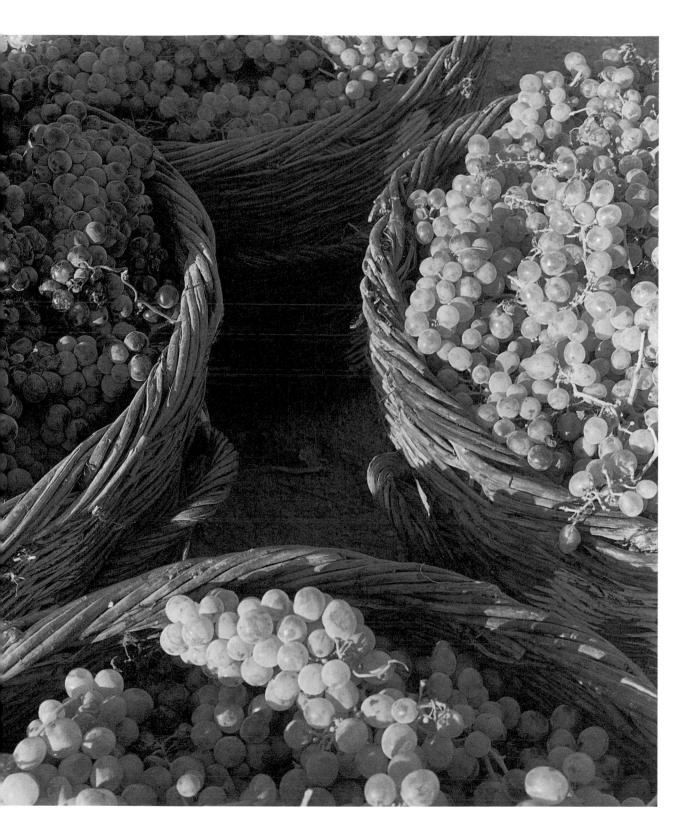

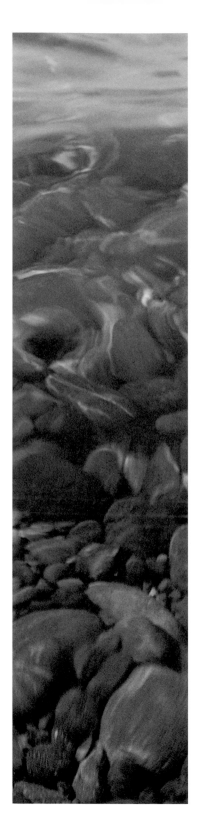

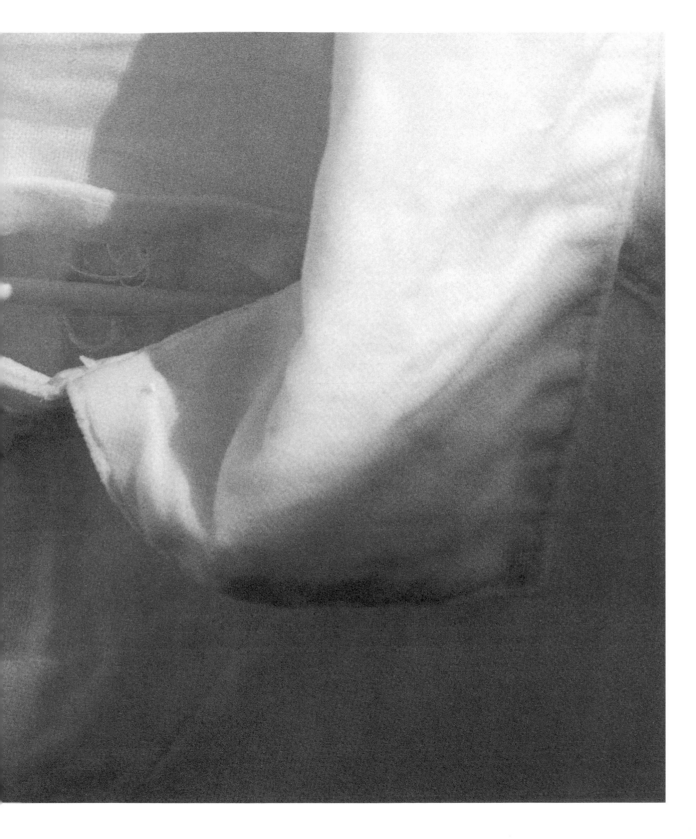

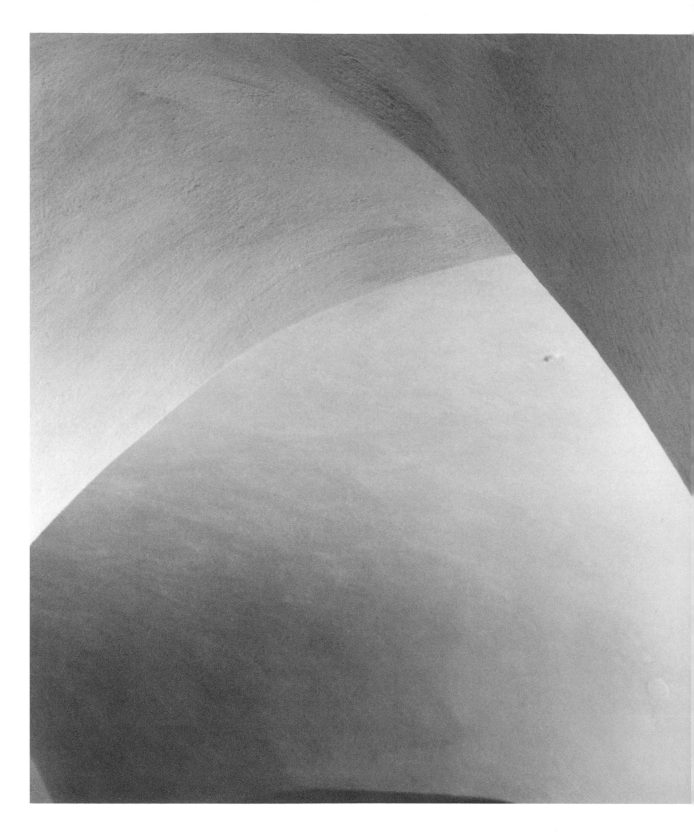

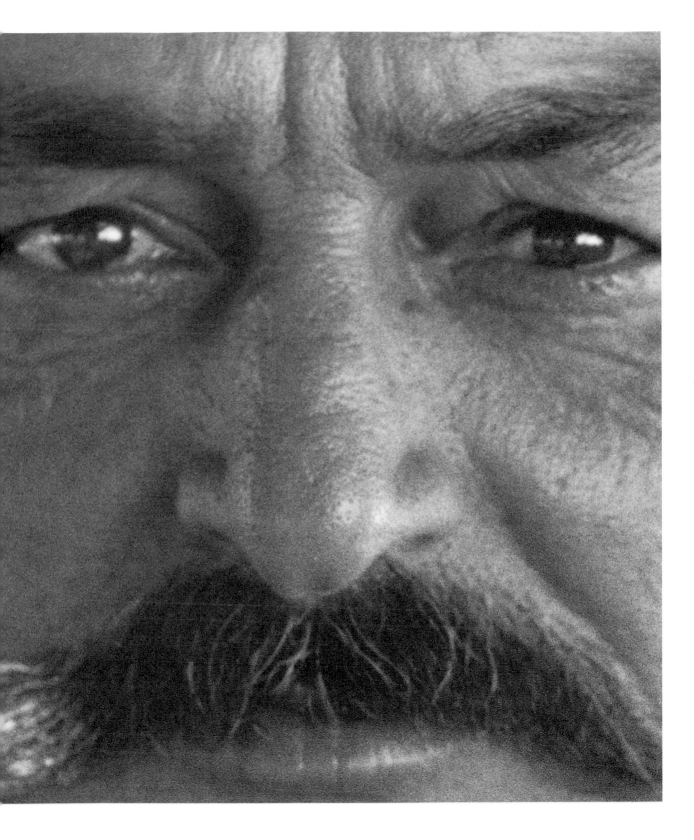

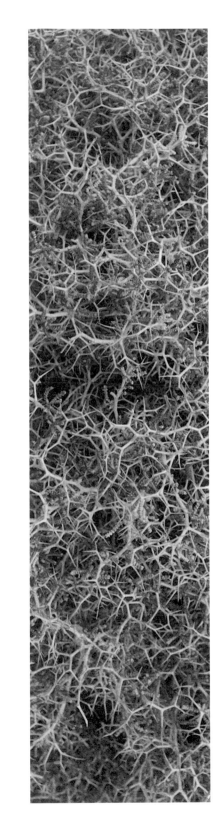

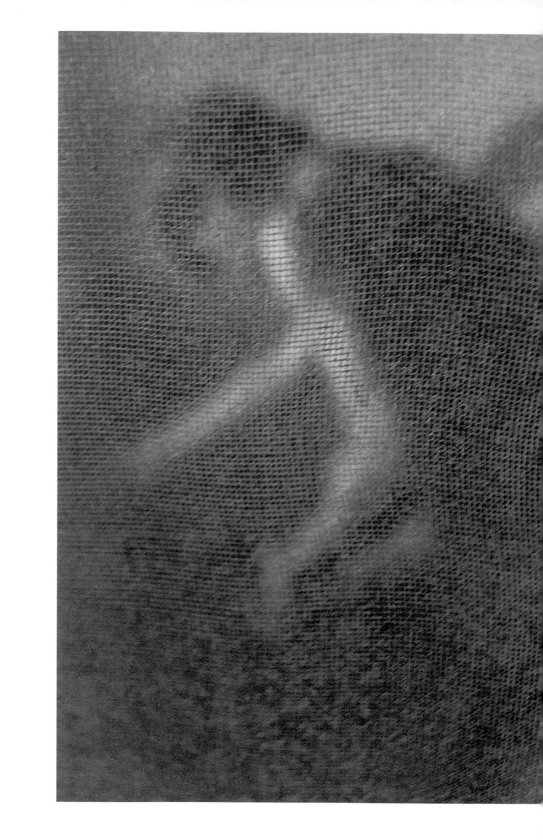

.

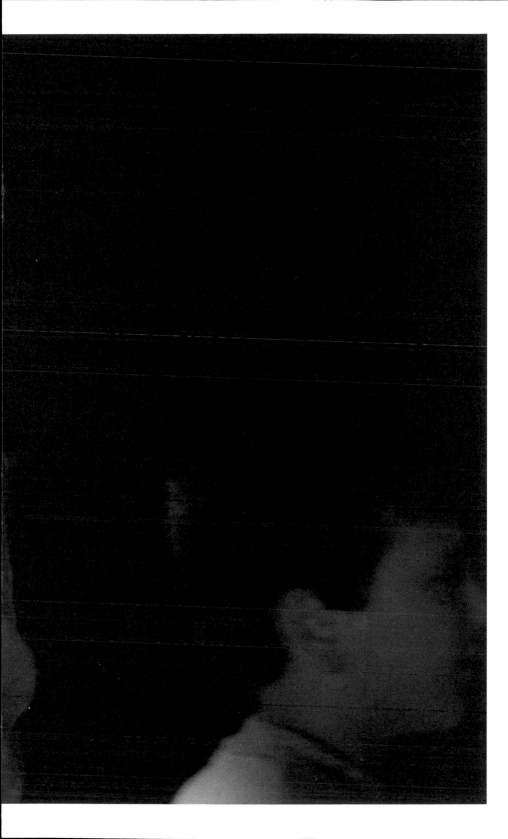

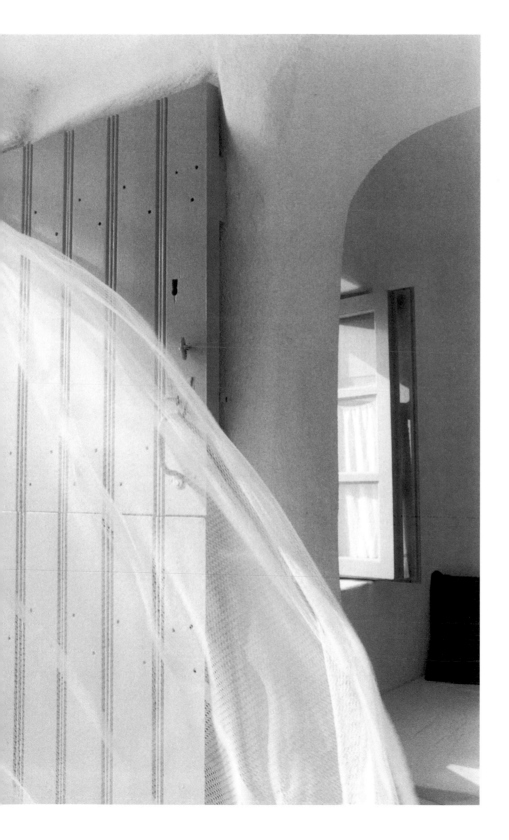

Index of Photographs

Aegina, 1992

Patmos, 1991

Santorini, 1991

Patmos, 1991

Sifnos, 1990

Santorini, 1995

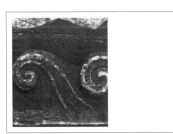

Thassos, 1992

Aegina, 1996; Patmos, 1991

Patmos, 1991

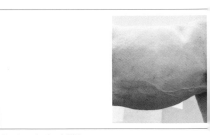

Santorini, 1991

Naxos, 1990; Karpathos, 1998

Santorini, 1991; Tinos, 1991

Naxos, 1992

Sifnos, 1992

Santorini, 1988

Patmos, 1991

Naxos, 1990; Santorini, 1988

Tinos, 1991; Karpathos, 1997

Naxos, 1990

Santorini, 1992

Santorini, 1989

Sifnos, 1990

Santorini, 1991

Tinos, 1991

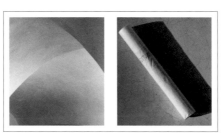

Santorini, 1989; Santorini, 1990

Sifnos, 1990

Patmos, 1991

Santorini, 1989

Naxos, 1990

Naxos, 1990

Aegina, 1992; Halki, 1990

Santorini, 1990

Santorini, 1998

Andros, 1997; Santorini, 1991

Karpathos, 1997; Karpathos, 1998

Tinos, 1991

Santorini, 1989

Tinos, 1991

Santorini, 1998

Tinos, 1991

Karpathos, 1998; Santorini, 1998

Tinos, 1991

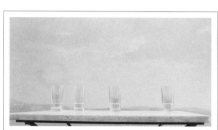 

Santorini, 1992

Tinos, 1991; Tinos, 1991

Naxos, 1990

Santorini, 1990

Santorini, 1998

Santorini, 1991

Santorini, 1988

Santorini, 1991; Santorini, 1991

Santorini, 1989

Santorini, 1995; Santorini, 1991

Sifnos, 1990

Tinos, 1991

Santorini, 1991

Santorini, 1998

Aegina, 1992

Santorini, 1998

Santorini, 1991

Santorini, 1991; Karpathos, 1998

Santorini, 1990

Sifnos, 1990

Santorini, 1990

Naxos, 1999

Patmos, 1991; Delos, 1991

Hydra, 1996

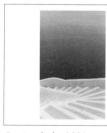

Santorini, 1991

Symi, 1998

Santorini, 1995

Santorini, 1992

Santorini, 1988

Thirrassia, 1992

Mykonos, 1996; Santorini, 1991

Naxos, 1990; Santorini, 1991

Santorini, 1989

Santorini, 1988

Acknowledgments

During the sixteen years I was photographing for this book, many people lent me caring support, time, and expertise. Prime among those people is my friend and wife, Andrea Raisfeld. Her encouragement, unending love, and frank critiques kept me focused, positive, and inspired. Without her, I would have left this project long ago. My children, Zander, Simon, and Max Athena gave me understanding on nights when I was late to dinner or away traveling.

Special thanks to: my agents Becky Lewis and Jaesoon Choi, Anne Kennedy, Carol Leflufy, Brica Wilcox, and everyone at Art and Commerce, New York; Vincent Simonet and Amelie De Andreis at Art and Commerce, Paris; Kathleen Klech, Yolanda Edwards, Lucy Gilmour, Dana Nelson, Tom Wallace, and the *Condé Nast Traveler*, which provided me with many opportunities to return to these islands; Marta Hallett, Elizabeth Viscott Sullivan, and Signe Bergstrom at Rizzoli International Publications, Inc.; Sarah Lazin and Corey Halaby at Sarah Lazin Books; my family at Perivolas in Oia, Santorini: Yannis Papadakis, Costis, Marie Irini, Nadia and Valontia Psychas, Emma Salmon, Timos Tsoukalas, Lina Vyse, and Molly Morton; Tom Baril; Leonard Benowich; Bonni Benrubi; Leonard Cohen and Kelley Lynch at Leonard Cohen Stranger Music; Evelyn Daitz; Stephen Doyle; Richard Ferretti; Peter Frank; Adam Glassman; Laura Harrigan; Edmund Keeley; Robert O'Connell; Sally Schneider; Suzanne Shaker; Suzanne Slesin; Martha Stewart; Gael Towey; Joy Aubrey, Diana DeMaria, Bruce Frizzell, Suzanne Saylor, and Indira Wiegand at Exhibition Prints; my assistants, Natasha Brien, Tom Holton, Laura Moss, Sara Mulhearn, Jason Schmidt, and Chante Tenoso; Dennis O. Palmore and New Directions Books; Agence Hoffman; Antonia Lakis, who put it all in order and made it dance; and, especially, my mentor and friend, George Tice.

Filakia, Filoi Mou...

First published in the United States of America in 2001 by
RIZZOLI INTERNATIONAL PUBLICATIONS, INC.
300 Park Avenue South
New York, NY 10010

ISBN:0-8478-2328-8
LC:00-103992

Distributed by St. Martin's Press

Printed and bound in Singapore